OBLIGATIONS OF VOICE

By the same author:

Reading the Magnificat in Australia: Unsettling Engagements (2020)
On arrivals of breath (2019)
White on White (2018)
Il ricordo: Six days in Val Taleggio (chapbook, 2018)
hope for whole: poets speak up to Adani (ebook, 2018)
Intatto/Intact (with Massimo D'Arcangelo and Helen Moore, 2017)
Ecological Aspects of War: Engagements with Biblical Texts (with Keith Dyer and Deborah Guess, 2017)
Ecological Aspects of War: Religious and Theological Perspectives from Australia (with Deborah Guess and Keith Dyer, 2016)
This flesh that you know (chapbook, 2015)
Kin (2014)
Climate Change—Cultural Change: Religious Responses and Responsibilities (with David Gormley O'Brien, 2013)
Reinterpreting the Eucharist: Explorations in Feminist Theology and Ethics (with Carol Hogan, Kim Power and Claire Renkin, 2013)
The Matter of the Text: Material Engagements between Luke and the Five Senses (2011)
Bent toward the thing (chapbook, 2011)
Claimed by Country (chapbook, 2010)
Stolen Heath (chapbook, 2009)
An Ecological Feminist Reading of the Gospel of Luke: A Gestational Paradigm (2005)

OBLIGATIONS OF VOICE

ANNE ELVEY

RECENT
WORK
PRESS

Obligations of Voice
Recent Work Press
Canberra, Australia

Copyright © Anne Elvey, 2021

ISBN: 9780645008937 (paperback)

A catalogue record for this
book is available from the
National Library of Australia

Cover image: Tsvetoslav Hristov on unsplash
Cover design: Recent Work Press
Set by Recent Work Press

recentworkpress.com

SS

To Anne M Carson and Rose Lucas
in gratitude for your collegiality, poetry and
friendship during COVID-19 lockdown in
Melbourne 2020

Contents

PART 1: BREATHING OUT

PART 2: BRIEFLY SUDDENLY

PART 3 : TO WRITE THE WIND

PART 4: WHERE WE SLEEP

PART 1
BREATHING OUT

Winter writing

Air gathers into green, inhabits
each gap between leaves that cup
the cold. Nights begin too early, end

too late. My eyes close on a sentence
on a graphite word. A hexagonal shaft
loosens, falls from my fingers. I stir.

My thumb has pressed hard on the certified
wood, has covered the disclosure—MADE
IN GERMANY—printed in gold. I grasp

a childhood frisson: the page ready
for the mark. Steady. Go. Cold
tingles in my digits. Mortality

gives itself as freedom to commit
to the unfinished—like the deliberate
accident of this suburb and its scrub.

Grasp

Stippled hands
circumnavigate a dial

as if they were
windows on a mortal

infinity, the kind
a mathematician finds

countable. Trout
glisten under

corrugated water as it
clears—a shiver

of scale. You
try to recollect

the name—a scope
that threw out

rainbow curves
of sine, how

before that sliver
of near stars you

did not know distance
as chronology. It is

always the impossible.
Can a child pace out

a light year
knowing what packet

spills from astral
fires saying

we are nothing
but ourselves

Annie

the tennis court owning
neighbour's annie get your
gun shrunk me   could i

i'd hide amid grass
blades in that season   when
he stood complicit

with my father   two tanned
men in shorts and dunlops
returning an idea of mates

boys' taunt waterworks
was embarrassment by contrast
a man can strip you

with a name

After the reading

Return to the old case
the voice, to the leather case
shaped to a doll, the case

lined with crimson, the satin-
lined box, an unburnt

throat. Over the torso
fold the loose limbs
of the saying. Shut on itself

the wood jaw. Tilt
the slack neck. Take

the hand from under the skirt.
Tuck the cloth. Fit
to its shape the thing. Close

the quiet lid. Press
down the rusted clasps.

Afternoon tea, Seaford Beach Café

A woman stands

        at the back of a throat.

   Tonsils prickle

          her spine. Her tongue

is a hallway runner.

        Jaws open

to threadbare rain.

        Against light

  her gums are charcoal.

         Lower teeth

irregular

        with decay. Breath

  surges before

        the locomotion of sea. Dark

corrugations. Luminous

         steel. Her voice

  is drenched in salt.

        She is a lump

in the gullet. A skiff

          bounces on swell.

Dear Citizen X,

There's nothing I can do to frighten these
words into submission. The Empire tried
putting them in detention in Van Diemen's
Land but they mutated and have them-
selves spread across the mainland like
a virus, infecting other tongues. You might
think they have erased such victoriously.
They are transformed—nor can you tie them
to your meanings, *illegal* for instance as applied
to *maritime* not manifold *arrivals*. I am tattooing
a word on my forehead for a game. You must
guess who stitched *survival* into pursed
lips, who shredded *shame* on a barb
attempting to scale a perimeter, who
confounded *grace*. Do you give up?
You have seven letters and thirty seconds
to bingo—you score fifty bonus
points and may stay on the mainland
where, X, you may spend your days
recollecting your consent, the stupor of our polity,
the muteness of our unpicked mouths.

Sincerely,
A

Obligations of voice

over the urge
is a drive
that is not yours

*what is it
to open to place
unaware
of its taboos*

*what is it to speak
thanks to a leaf
to fancy that this
is something you can do*

*should you undo
your taking
to catch a breath
in your cinema of sleep*

over the bed
is a web
that is not yours

*do you hear wind
answer as if you
attend when presence
is your lie*

over the park
is a canopy
that is not yours

over the house
is a sky
that is not yours

over the day
is a breath
that is not yours

*whose ceremony
do you interrupt
striding your own
dimmed genius*

*what is it
to evade the here
of keeping by those
who walk the land*

over the path
leans a paperbark
that is not yours

*what do you see
through a scratched
lens in your
laboratory of guess*

over eyes' blur
is a social
that is yours

*does your shame
spill
sacred
into a trap*

over your garden
is a theft
that is yours

*why do you compost
what you collect
though you still
do not grasp*

over your stockpile
is a cloud
that is yours

*what do you buff
or mantle or with worm
build a soil as if
never to refrain*

over your voice
a duty
that is given

Pollination

Roads interrupt ramble where your sign
is an LA flicker and white taste tops

a hill. The build breathes, as if the artisan
were made for matter, though finitude is

misdirected when scarcity lies. Enough
energy and flesh have been usurped. You begin

again intestate. A buzz of calling is diverted
by casual stifling. You sing the urgency of doing

nothing. The comb you stole drips. Your
buds recall an intercept of kindness. Passing.

Storm parable

Breath of a wing
                              brushes
        against a Bren. Dawn arrives   as a last post is

                                        delivered before promise
        of rain. Beads
                        spill from grey.

A pool
                now pitted
                                lies in guts   where mercy lives.

        Once a father   dashed from his gate when shame   came home.
Ute's dust-trail   marks
a return.

                Where are the mothers of daughters? a church sculptor asks.
A man laughs
at the extravagance

of gravel
                tossed up.   A woman
retreats.   Did

her track
    improve politically with a
                        whisper?   She hunts

                                for what comfort recollection
                can bring.   When is party membership
a false walk?   Tears

                break on the cheeks of her election.

Words, words,
                words

                        past their meanings unhinge
                                        the history of the idea.
Propaganda is stomp

                and song   and claws
                on her roof.   What happens again
        is disappointment.   Will her line

forgive chance   when even prophets
                                snub   an encroaching sea?
                        A woman and a girl read *The Tempest* with a strange

accomplice. Auden's Ariel
                        bends
                time.   Afterwards   the woman

                                                bumps into
        Caliban. He's been with Porter   writing Jonah
at a whale's behest.

Emergency

1

Snowmelt

Mind keeps
an index of flakes
a jindabyne of evidence
in an icy creek

Old habits
spill
over mossed files

2

Rocks
are keyed to the rapids
of imagination

3

In a rising lake
speed signs
are semi-submerged

4

In the Reef
graffiti surprises

It is a wash out

Greyscale
of organisms
whitening

Catch of breath
as scientists weep

In apocalypse

April 2020

In that dawn night   an orange morning came
  as charcoal sky. Two children masked
                              with mum.
Their small craft.

                    The remote took charge of the day
      as we sat
            like effigies of ourselves
                              bound

to Vic Emergency
                              though our guise
      remained in its package
                              against the haze

as it waits
            for hazard deferred. We run
on the spot   soap up and
                        sluice   learn again

a dispensation   of self.
                        In quartered turn
we discard our veneer.
                        It is old play

we are
      jigsawed in proximity
                              alone.
      Skirting

          the neighbours
                        on an evening walk
      our love song   in apocalypse
                              is quiet talk.

Called up

around 1970 i wondered

        would i be brave enough to be
        a conscientious

        objector   in mind i was

a youth who might be
an aeronautical

engineer or a pilot
    in liturgical dress trading
    for souls   i studied

        the underside
        of leaves   lay below
        unhurried

        cumulus   my father

on reading the intro to a book i
admired

said approvingly

      she writes
      like a man   i glowed

        in solidarity at
        the compliment and spilt

    tears

    at a priest's
    first mass   could i too have
        been chasubled

        raising bread above

                                                            a crown   bell
                for ear   there's a signal

                    in silence   my grandmother
            declared   i can smell
    the rain coming   three

                                        generations of mothers
                                            and daughters on the back
                                                porch   it came   now

    there's a name for it
                ground reaches toward
    desire   *petrichor*   i

                                    specie into place
                                        beside a creek
                    they returns

    to singular and slips   a
                downy child   between
    thighs   once

    i said to a therapist i feel
                like a man in a woman's
    body   trying it on   afterbirth

                                            splatters on the cannots
                membranes
    grow plumes

    i think about charity
                as if faith and hope
    were empty staves

                            such a music is
                    withheld   as other eyes work

women   what if

               that enchantment
                    with an egret
          had been requited

She says

                        a grassed stretch
between apartments   and Swan
                        seated in shade
    (where a wagtail courts her)   she wishes
for the sleep
                of seasons   her old burnout has
woken   so
                she says   home
is a page number missed
a finger scroll
    (wagtail is still courting)
                she says   tomorrow
is cousined stone
                        fingers cupped around
a succulent bloom
                    in vermillion
and greyscale   with all the letters of a name
dispersed   she says   it's a
bell   brought from Kent or   a tower
        Uno (you know)
    rocking and tumbling   by the quay

Increasing humidity

South Townsville, May 2019

eleven lines at 77%

i'll be attending a conference on
    transient transcendence   my son
tells me   this poetry of mathematics
        while i overhear wind-grade
of frond   against
    frond   as picks up to a city
ear   the sound
            of rain   or gravel
            raked   this business
            of tropical excess
                            and dry

twelve lines at 84%

what is not told
                un-coming
history shared
                yet stolen
    where   red
    leaves are not   autumnal
        but sultry splurge
of hue   of size   spilt
    glow   as water
sprays   palm fronds
yellowing   a lost
                when

thirteen lines at 91 %

night   that curlew cry
        like a cat trapped
or alarmed   a girl   and by day
    men   *though not all of you*
    big men   pale   (like me)
    they look   across a street
        or from a ute
each time it is   two   men
the shiver in this heat
        of go-inside
        secure   in any case
we were probably already
safe   though not all of us

fourteen lines at 98%

in the garden i see two   speckled
drongos   their sheen   their split
tails   confidence
    around me
    as an eagle   hovers
    over   ross creek
        i give an ear to
all this plenitude   in need
        of water   lately
flooded   and spooked by
    mould   residents are
    turned   trauma-wise
though not all of them
                and climate numb

An abyss of feathers

shunted
  through curvatures
of thought her
glance crosses currents with
  her smile (a
daddy's voice) her eyes
  pinched briny with
blur as (he

describes
  a bougain-
villea trailed
around a station in the north)
  she genuflects
before a squid's
  bath inking
consultations with

what saves
  (bureaucrats
and time?) beyond
which is this welcoming
  abyss of
feathers fragrant
  with another
tenure (the

possessive
  renounced for
enthralment) when each
dapple of sunlight
  will be her
signifier for the
  loosening thighs
of her pith

Natality

body's habitude begins
with buoyancy, a saturated skin

and musculature that urges toward
this interface with air insisting itself

inward, prompting a cry.
it is a complex exercise of flesh

this chemistry and bellows, this ear
to tongue, whatever bids.

mud pies. hands gloriously
soiled. they find their ends in play

Breathing out

Scrub is salt and ragged across the conglomerate ground. Blue arcs over teal. The water is almost calm. Her laptop is closed. She has put away her avatars. A day moon rises with frail light. A boat is moored at the base of the cliff. She sloughs off monitors and canisters, masks and tubes. Cirrus frays from a dressing. On a bench she sits on names cut deep. Paint peels, olive. Her bones are vulnerable to cold. Thin as rice paper, her skin is talc. The pulse is improvised, rapid, slow. She was not a great lover of jazz. A child laughs in the shallows. Ants carry crumbs. The fringe of a sheoak is a gown in a draught. This is her debut. She catches her breath in her hands, opens them to the breeze. Arriving in slow motion, a pelican breaks the bay's surface to feed.

PART 2

BRIEFLY SUDDENLY

Body as tree

argent tendrils lift
coarse from brow   the incline

tipped with chill and sentience
a divine ire written   as if

taught by nose   or
history's small tightenings

hands have white
vestiges of   oven dish

new knife   a scald
witnesses disintegration

as focus blurs around
careers like banksia   with

every cone worked for
each resolve   sprung

Each cell cultivates its neighbours

Her plaits were rigorous though the seat ground when the two-wheeler careened over stone. All summer the soil was tight. The sky. The air. Like a griddle. *Mirror to mirror to receding squares—my father drafts a sketch for a cube.* Her ribbon came undone. Thorns laddered her hose. Blooms gave their name to fingered prayer. *Dimensions are subtracted, he teaches, to the plane.* Oh, how could she convince the future to behave? *His mother's name brings me to Cork.* She dreamt a pebble above a crater. Rare as a bible sprouting from spinifex, her tears pocked soil the shade of blood. *The flight is late.* Rain-washed, her stone gleamed charcoal and ash. A hint of pearl. Her terraced mind sank into her gut. *Irish beer is on the house.* She climbed, ladder by ladder. *At 3am the hire desk is open. The car nudges through murk.* Her body dropped to grass, her eyes fixed on forest, spine toward deep. *Feet wet in the Atlantic I read of famine and blight.* She mourned a svelte life dressed in off-cuts of chiffon, obedient to the wind. *Shingle and spud of chance—colleagues make angels in the long spring grass.* Tourists with children crashed into her grief. She had no option but to be altered matter, obligatory preserve. *Against the jamb on the white-wash cottage of generations leaving, I lean.* She strode over sunlit lawn, the air loud with birds. *I cannot compass the Tralee romance of the rose.* Grevillea burst. She was a net, strained around a cluster of marbles, holding against their mass.

Treasure hunt

Silver glints in the tea-tree. A clue is wrapped in foil, peeled from the lining of the cigarette pack and rolled into balls. The clue says, *look behind the beach hut.* Rosaries clack as sister strides through the yard. The bell swings with her right arm. A boy's hands are full of paper. *Ten paces from the chapel a blue cape.* On Sunday afternoon we play monopoly. I land on community chest. *That's Victor's dog,* Dad says. A Jack Russell explores the walkers and wheels. *When I was a boy,* Dad tells me, *I made treasure hunts for the other children. What was the treasure?* I ask. *There was never any treasure.* Sister Gertrude sees his cuffs are frayed, singlet and shirt tucked into his shorts, his socks pulled up in shoes he gives a lick and polish at the gate. Five boys and a girl gather. *Once upon a time,* Joe says, *there was a rider on the moor and mist hung all around. A bird called out a single note and nettles stung.* The bell. Dad lies in bed. The TV shows an old war movie. *We used to watch Saturday matinees,* I say. *Hmpph,* says he. *Forgive me,* she says, as she bustles past in the corridor tight with dinner carts and walkers. *She's a nice one,* Dad says, *likes my little funnies.* Dining, Dad sips chardonnay. *We'll get there,* he says. Joe writes on the back of an old composition. At lunch, *a horse whinnies on the moor.* Water pools in the asphalt and the shoes. *Joe, Joe,* a boy yells, *I found a clue: under our lady's toe, the crushed head of the snake. I got it Joe. I got it! How many clues are there? I can't wait to see the treasure.* A personal attendant admires the picture on his wall: beach huts in a yellow light. *I painted that,* Dad says, *forty years ago. For an hour today,* he tells me, *they left me in the corridor. I used to be top of my class,* Jim says. *Jim's lost it,* says Dad. The virgin's foot covers a clue. The wattle's gold hides another. *We'll get there,* Joe tells the children who eat clues for lunch. His mother leaves the church with mop and broom. Sister Gertrude drops a few coins in her hand. *A grey shawl hangs on the moor all day. I might be a modern-day Dickens,* he writes. Under the crocheted rug at the foot of the bed, the gap for a toe is a word that just escaped him. *We'll get there,* Dad says. Small fingers wrap clues in silver foil.

Christmas after all

There's nothing more to do except to say *be kind* as you hang the Animals Australia ornament on the tree, to sing the species of recovery, the thing you dread. Refusal of a bite, spider hanging from the fly wire of the back door, ads for sprays of all kinds—Jonah waits to be written. His poem is swallowed and thrown up by a porter on a foreign beach. A ball boy ready to fetch another's misplaced shot accounts for stardom. You contemplate the hubris of health, as if this might not all end transformed—matter for matter for matter, soil with its biota like a living AI. You've nothing to lose.

I'm not ready she said last week.

It's too late she said the week before.

Let me go to her house, find her nativity set and arrange it on the chest of drawers in her rehabilitation room, as if it were Christmas after all.

A black swan

In these moments the air rings and death walks about the garden like a
pigeon who picks through dry leaves by day or a possum that clatters each
night across the tiles. Then the globes are neon and the TV's black box
clunk-whirrs on record. There are flights—stairs and wings, the ascent
of years like a gospel's close or acts that open—as if we might have made
a difference in the chance of being

other

wise. A parent lies

in the aloneness of delirium and—as if Alexis Wright
had summoned it—a black swan seemingly glides (webbed feet paddling
hard unseen) on Port Phillip Bay, not far from the Seaford shore

just north of McCulloch Avenue

and the new boardwalk

through the scrub. Then all that tames what might have been is now
and gone—

a mortal taming
of the wild accident
of love.

Birth

Soft caul—
this skin
across the
crown is

slack.
Fluid held
against this
form

spills. I
breathe the
space of
time. Squat.

My partner
bolsters
me. The
midwife

holds a
mirror. Amid
surges I
see a

grey thing—
corrugated
flesh. It
stretches me

then retreats
a gasp. There's
blood and shit
and water.

I burn. A
sudden
pressure. World
stills.

Between my
thighs your
scream
slides.

The second time

I thought it would be
easier. So the books said.

Instead there was my
body

out of time. On all fours
naked. Heaving. Orang-utan arse

blooming. Belly
swayed. Mind

was numb
with fear you would be

stillborn. Gutters of grey bound the tiled white
of the floor. I was a massive piece

on your first game board. Rules were a
nonsense. A stark

light surrounded me though flesh knew
it was night. Like waves

in a lab tank where curious
a student

placed a small block and ball
pain came without

pattern. My partner
held together in another place

beside me. My skin
shrieked *do not touch* while

the midwife wore a button
that read

condoms are a girl's best friend.
Sometime after midnight

she said *I'm going now*
you'll find your way.

Her words made space
in me. Steady.

Breakers took shape toward shore.
Minutes

then or hours you
appeared.

There was some fuss about the cord.
Tide stilled, I saw you

for the first time.
Did I think or speak the words?

This
is the most beautiful thing I've ever seen.

Night gusts with house and flowering gum

after Omar Sakr, 'What It Is To Be Holy', in The Lost Arabs

In the billow   of the pre-midnight quarter hour
          I put aside my book
                         having recovered the holy in sense.
     Flesh

          is a genuflection before the immense
     tangle of history
                    in bodies that seek the solace
                                        of tact.   I spill

into sleep's   missed stitch.   Now every possum
          is awake   in the canopy   like a child
     persuading a parent.   Into the curl of recall   I fold
the forget.

                    Remedy   takes off on the wind
                                        like a ban   the white
                    shopping bag
                              breath-filled   not quite   alive.

Skin world

These things break
to feeling—the sister's

limbs in myoclonic
seizure, the parent's

delirium, the coast's
erosion in the king

tide, the body's
flesh. The body's

memory of event
where skin

and world fuse.
The self is rent

by yes, by the makings
of toward, the face

that calls—a summons
in the interstices

of becoming (she gulps
as her limbs engage—

her father called it
a fling) like a wound.

Staying with the Grey Sisters
at age 3¼

In the inchoate umber of a May
cot, up against water

piping heat, autumn
chills the silence of her daddy's

squeeze. Sirens box
the night like absent love

that a child paints
as tree. Red leaves

scatter at its base. Who can
ease the crying days?

When she asks, a lesson is
denied. A coif covers

power as it switches and
she stands up in bed—

a mimic of containment—while
a small fly butts

a pane that's specked with strikes.
Floor's polish shrills

with sin and a visit disallowed.
Everywhere is the drear beige

of things she cannot be
as she reaches for it all.

Without you

to hear the chatter by eye as if through a pane
to strike matchgirl lights for consolation

to escape a gut   swoop like prayer   wings wide
to develop old film
                                physic   chemical   eye
    aperture

to become (without you) the thing
                                        it requires
    a plant growing by its own light

                                    at a cliff's turn toward
                                    a petrified forest   stride
                                    is a pastorate of sorts

    wearing nan's ring   of vocation
                her idiom of disillusion

Distant calculations

1

Spill of a son's held hand and mind, tuned by number to code that dances
in centuries from east and west, maps silent imaginaries and stars—hardly
a tangible.

2

He left for France, not with trench helmet or tin cup but thought of
graphs, planar pedestrians and Douglas Adams, our 70s science entangled
with silly walks and Poincaré, whose fantastic lack of a dimension seems
like Britain's script from Monty who skip-hops away.

3

A circus clown cannot fly. Lockdown has me climbing Lombardy past
Vendesi signs. My partner is playing table tennis across language in the sun.
From Milano to Gare du Nord, the slow train is skirting worlds.

4

In midwinter Melbourne, the Tour ascends *le mont*. Chateaux and woods
reel by. They are easing something in me, as a novel strain extends.

5

Sunday night Skype, the lad's just out of bed, breakfasting, and well. On
boardgamearena.com we play *7 Wonders*. Science is mapping the limits of
viral arithmetic—such *terrible beauty*.

6

The air clears and then it does not. The composer inserts climate data into their score.

7

Protests are muted by the daily toll. Thefts I live with live beyond my calculation. Do I imagine otherwise? There is no vaccine against complicity. Let treaty come.

Things fall away

the moment a tree
consoles with its rooted

                stem that
                    stands and asserts what
                    you also bear

toward
      the coherence of earth.
                A mutual ken

                        crosses species   between

     things that travel
and things that stay

                in place. Leaves
                    give wind
                        its multiple voice

as they shift
your long recollection
                of a soul's green

night. You are again
                a girl. Skip
         Skip

          Skip the tor
on the pavement.   Hop
              Hop

                Hop over chalked
lines. You retreat
from old need.

A dog rests
her head in your
lap. A magpie

seems to know

how you feel
about song.

Grevillea Robusta

i.m. Deborah Bird Rose

Spines curve. Scores of digits are
                          gold tucked
                                    in branch-work.
            Rain draws blood
                          from brawny gum that stands

beside three townhouses, new behind our block, with their too-neat grass
laid out and watered in. Bay beaches after storm-filled nights are closed.
Hoary fish, half-buried in creek's sediment, are gone. Parents watch their
magpie young.

                    Writing still toward shimmer
            your days
                    fall like salt
                          while children hold out
                                    for planetary kindnesses. Wind gathers

            about our speaking house of tin
            and thud, footsteps of limbs splayed
            against a flue—each thing's
            sprung turn toward relation

a communion that is yes, you taught,
    across a wound's resolution, saying
                          what gilt filigree declares to feeding birds,

                    Come.

Briefly suddenly

i.m. Martin Harrison

slightly cheaply   suddenly simply seriously

occasionally   distantly
slowly   nearly recently   finally

usually mostly perfectly
occasionally consciously

nearly daily

    only only   entirely entirely

apparently frantically   really quietly

differently   simply listlessly   carelessly
newly   already loosely   mostly early
sincerely   only   only

suddenly suddenly   invisibly   suddenly

differently   definitely

probably   nearly likely   nervously   only usually
already practically   only

momentarily   blindly
mostly suddenly   absently

clearly   scarcely secretly
                          invisibly invisibly

hardly   already already   fleetingly   only

exquisitely eternally

PART 3
TO WRITE THE WIND

Gusts at evening

on BoonWurrung Country (Seaford, Victoria)

                        Brooms
of eucalypt   are
              in their sweep   herding
                                    atmosphere.
                                                Night's
            tipping ebb
                    and surge   of air

            is a hatch of time
                        spoken
                                                as paws
tread onto gumnuts

                        damp and shaken

                            from limb
                            and deed.
Shielded from squall is
                                    the fiction of title.
A trickle soothes and stings.

                    Waters   fresh
                and salt
                        are parting.   Even now   they are
        kind and   fleet.

Demeter and Persephone

after Igor Stravinsky, Perséphone *and* Le Sacre du printemps

Each chorister holds
    at a slight angle
        the score
so that two tiers of white edges
        resemble
  a flock of gulls
    in flight.

  Male voices
     intone a journey   to the depths
    and back.
        Then choirs
         of girls and boys
      with a women's chorus

  sing the soaring trail
       of mother's desire
       for daughter
           fixed
  in patriarchal tug

or worse.
     What escape was her first
   descent?
        Is it trauma now   that pulls her
under earth again   or what she
        consumed?

  That red pomegranate
      or mother's blood
   spilt?

  Does her milk

recover her child?   The
                                                      Fall

was not her fault.   Shame
                                unfurls
its   silver   plumes

                          escapes into   light
  where she
              may smell again
                          the spring
      when she clambers
          through

                          friable ground   toward
            her earthen   her azure
                                              dome.

Eden

she tastes the ab-
surd   the square root of a number that is not a perfect square

she writes herself
into the diction of a sunset   when the overcast west blushes with lemon

she investigates hard
rubbish and the scent of jasmine   and startles three lorikeets from the apple

she remembers lilac
a breast grazed   in the laundry-yard

she notes that the knees
of her Sunday pants are worn   sometimes

she finds the vowels
missing   from the script

she fills the irrational
spaces   between the more readily-defined of the reals

she notices that sentences
have become threadbare   only fit for rags

she tosses them
into a basket   wafers feigning bread   she is the cloth

she unpegs and folds
roughly for cleaning   a thing too worn for wearing

she writes the mod
of heaven thus |heaven| equates it with a forest or art   a material artefact

she needs a sign
between less than and greater than   equal to the singing in her soul

she wakes to hear
a transcribed angel would sound the same   in paradise

her eden may be an electronic foxhole   or the place from which
she writes

Memorial coin

A rainbow of magic possums
plays ring-a-rosie
on the $2 coin she

passes for the boat ride to
freedom saying listen
listen to me listen

           to the swell of the torn
           sea circling
           detention. Her words slice an infant's

           skull like an egg
           soft-boiled, knife into
           mind dips, as if a soldier

into yolk. The wall of
Dumpties keeps toxic
compact with truth. Ask

Pilate his proper
tag. Ask what's in a
name. Hear him counter, what is

Trump? All
the Duttons are sitting on
fences looking up

           synonyms for detention.
           Roget says, try
           kidnapping. When a detainee

           falls, she is crying
           no one else treats me
           the way you do. It's not a

compliment. With the sea
between duress and roiling
words, her bum presses

into sand. A coin
washes up. She
buries it beside her shoe.

Recollection

Le Nozze di Figaro seems to follow
her disposition. Coriander seeds
fry with cumin

and cloves of garlic
crushed, curative gratings
of turmeric, ginger, ginger
ginger, the fragrance
of elevation like opera or

three wheelchairs fitting in an airport
lift. Her muscles remember
their weight. This curry

of encounter is a comb to
hide. She touches
lavender water to her
pulse, her ear tuned
to annunciation. Later

she speaks with a refugee
of home as felled tree and the leave-
taking, when spitfires

mass in tumbled leaves.
Together they load a broken
table into a Ute. Marsupials
are stirring. A talisman
of theft alights

from the tail of an airbus. She
recalls standing on a jetty
on a prison island, thinks a name

Sarah.

Location location location

a shifting margin
pivots on desire
to assimilate under
the purview of theorists
who say *the goodies are for
the earning   publishing
is our real estate*

texts incise
a colleague says
efface bodies
matter   too
though script
is a gulp drawn
to signal this

shift of white
curve like anime
in the fold of a creek
still and alert
brighter than blooms
of tea tree near
the bridge from whence

determined pace
marks out what
comes   becomes
gust gale
squall   hands
pocketed   tongue
tied on cliché

plastic flurries
each day assume
their currents   paths
of shimmer and smog
(this load of lift)
marled parchment
in colonial clench

Refugee outtake

They are lining up in security gear with their calculators
        on jetties that jut
                from back gardens in Patterson Lakes

to divide 65 million according to capacity to learn
        the global fraction
                of a person they need to turn away

through an artificial drained wetland. Ignorance
        blunders on that
                disinheritance—malicious or not

the effect is the same. Kindness is the bluntest
        instrument they
                retreat from, guesting the impossible.

Police are texting the slippage of souls between egret,
        dock and space
                as Venus stands out against a deepening.

Thumbs up for a No News Day said the wattlebird

nothing   and yet
the said of a tree

where a wattlebird
shrieks that   there's

nectar at the hub
of   a spiked bloom

scarlet as a signal for
emergency   and soft

like time slowed
to the pace   of a moral

missed when all at
once   apocalypse

arrives in desiccations
that had seemed   deferred

no news which is not
fake news   but this

scorching of control
another   *hottest day*

on record   when conscience
mollified is   trumped

and peachy   *how good*
is a parliament of guess

while wind again says
gum   and on cue

a wattlebird   replies

(Un-)domesticated settlement

TAMED   BY   BLOND   '50S
BRICK-VENEER™   HER   DAMP
RISES   THROUGH   BOARDS   FROM
SWAMP   AND   GUST
CYCLES   IN   POSSUM-HAUNTED   GUMS
BOSCH™   CHURNS   THE   HOUSEHOLD
SNOW   PARLIAMENT™
JELLIES   HATE   ON   THE   TV™
AND   SHE   PINS   UP   HER
NOSTALGIA   FOR   LONG-HAIRED
BEADS   OR   BEARDED   JEANS
LEGO™   OF   A   MORATORIUM
MECCANO™   OF   REFERENDA
AS   IF   POLITY   WERE   EASY   LIKE
RAISING   A   CHILD?   AS   IF
RESISTANCE   WERE   EFFICIENT   AS
CAPACITY   WHERE   BILLS   PAY   THEM-
SELVES   IN   A   KENWOOD™   WORLD
HER   TINNITUS   IS   A   BAMIX™
OR   A   STORY   DROWNED   BY
SELF-ABSORPTION   PROCESS™
IS   MARKING   TIME   WHEN
HER   CUPBOARD   OPENS   IN
A   DRAUGHT   IS   COMFORT™
WHAT   KEEPS   HER
SETTLED™   BESIDE   A   BROKEN
PEG   WHERE   THE   KITES   OF   HISTORY™
ARE   LYING   WINDLESS   AT   HER
FEET?   SHE   PUTS   ON
ANOTHER   LOAD   HANGS   IT
UNDER   SKY   AND   GULLS
A   CESSNA™   PASSES
OVER   HER   BRANDING   CULT
WHILE   NATION™   BURNS

At Cana watching Dan and Brett while listening to Michael Farrell read

My mother is in an aged care facility.
There are duelling press conferences this week.
Farrell is on at 11am.
Poetry is reading water as wine.
Politeness is looking through the glass.
A plough is transubstantiating a paddockful of thefts.

The shaft is using indentured labour.
Coronavirus is in Mum's home.
There's a rabbit at the window.
There are duelling press conferences this week.
Memory is littered with dead kangaroos.
Dan and Brett are on at 11am.

Dan is answering a question about Eid.
'Cos white settlers never do the wrong thing.
I am thinking about consolation as political protest.
My mother is having lunch from disposable crockery.
There are duelling press conferences this week.
Aunty says it hasn't yet reached 10 degrees in Seaford.

The dead horse is tattooed into the family hillside.
Dan is waiting on advice.
There are duelling press conferences this week.
There are no miracles on Covid-19 ground.
Arthritis fumbles plastic cutlery.
Mary is advising on the proper hospitality for nuptials.

Poetry is reading water as wine.
Politeness is looking through the glass.
A third testing was yesterday.
Masks are results.
A plough is transubstantiating a paddockful of thefts.
There are duelling press conferences this week.

There are duelling press conferences this week.
Memory is littered with dead kangaroos.
It is possible to listen to two things at once.
Zoom is served in full PPE.
Dan is answering a question.
Dear Jesus, I am calling my mum.

Coronavirus is giving a press conference.
Farrell is on at 11am. Water is reading poetry.
The dead horse is tattooed on a miracle of ground.

Chortle

The engine was named *Chortle* without reason and its eleven carriages clung like the beginning of a world.

In that world no one could think the word *serf*. There was no expansion toward the kind of obedience that sub-serves. There was

an ear to the vibration of impending things should time, too, lay down its one-way track.

Was there sentiment? The possibility of affection, energy toward other energy, letting go so as to open toward unimaginable alterities?

The great elastic enterprise of matter was sharpening its *esse* on bonds that to the lay mind are ephemeral at best.

She put down her pen. What would *Chortle* do with its eleven carriages and lofty likeness to the universe?

To write the wind

to attempt the impossible   write

wind   shows itself in the limb
curved for the sun to catch a cluster of leaves for the shadows

to hold themselves otherwise   say

wind   shivers through
the lances and shakes the rose

to inhabit their difference   see

wind   scatters gum nuts on the track
a branch snaps

to be inchoate   hear

wind   gives the
leaves voice

to answer an intent that's unfinished   imagine

wind   picks up hair around
a face   clouds move

to grasp nothing   think

wind   turns over and over   a dead
leaf clatters across the suburban   pitch

PART 4
WHERE WE SLEEP

Sacramental agnostic,
Mr Christian

I arrive by way of mutiny.
As second to the self's captaincy
I amend a creed in this squall.

Slops of Councils wash
from the tarred deck. This briny
world is a fictive place

I've never been
outside a tale of grizzled
tropes that signify fidelity

of a kind, or otherwise.
Everything's deep green
and lurching, alongside

an oceanic discipline
that feels a lot like chaos.
Sea is obedient

to an ancient rule, predating
humankind, predating bios.
The trick is to bear with it

or abstain: the able vessel's
deference to the swell
the body's nous for land.

Office

I dream an office gutted like a fish
that dies on our deck. The gloss of semi-
translucent flesh begins—like habit—
to fail. Sharp against the day's last

shadow and fire, the spine and finer
bones fall from the fisher's hand
to the boat's wake. They are the mariner's
leaf, floating shoreward on the tide.

Bare vertebrae are a church
a son—angled by a 'fisher of men'—
torched. Prayers are my cinders, charred
words my relics of integrated

circuits and main frames. My screen
no longer flickers with a prompt to save.

To the bookmaker god

With ticket and stub you are making a book
of this heart. My hand reads the ridges
on the pacer's spine and bindings whisper

in tongues. Roan of my favourite season
whickers like a fold in a leaf. With rustle
of silk, winter sun will canter the aisles

burnish the wood. All Saints and All Souls
will suspend days' trade. Spring carnival
done, I'll re-shelve the rhetoric of love

write for nothing else. I'll check
the Dewey for harness and bit, catalogue
turf with green and find your Cup in Stacks.

No more than must

On reading the Final Report of the Royal Commission into Institutional Responses to Child Sexual Abuse, Volume 16, Religious Institutions, Book 2, while on writing retreat, October 2018

1

I see the machine adjust by slow creep each cog shifts no more than must, no more than must to answer, to preserve a long dominion, as I read names I know of men with purple hose who whisky together, more real for them the snug of old boys' guild than the word of a child.

2

In the green grocer that day, I held my toddler, while the local priest admired his blond curls. From that priest's room, I'd heard another boy. I told my son *beware he's not a good man*, wishing instead I could teach trust.

3

Outside court years late, three clerics giggled like naughty kids, over a witness on a priest. *At least he didn't see anything*, one said. In the aisle amid produce as foot traffic passes, nearly thirty years on I'm holding my child.

4

Ubiquitous in evidence, this word *scandal* becomes a norm for abjuration. Discredit of each sacrament, a stumbling noun is eliding childhoods. The seal is already broken.

5

Her undergarments are wet beneath her dress and fear is a darkened closet,
its polished wood, when a child comes in to tell what was undone.

6

To shift and shift by will, to shift: a thousand, thousand collars dress in
hessian, ashes scatter over a thousand heads, outside their sanctuaries.
Absolution is no longer theirs to give.

7

What did lay not know in those days—a child threatened with hell, taught
to speak sins they did not own—*I disobeyed my parents*, *told a lie*—we
did not rebel, fed poison by trust, while rust has stiffened those gears no
creed is fit to *loose*.

8

In this genealogy of shame, my soul's exposure admits silence. Is it shock
or abdication?

Those who sow in tears ...

Psalm 126:5

1

Absorbed by the exercise
of syntax meeting
need, I strew

my pit and tread
less casually.
I list toward

account, a shaky
instance of pale.
Habit sows itself

in my tissue
as use enjoyed.
What ripens

exposes. My crop:
not to oblige but
to donate my bent.

2

As a thread tugged
is to a cat so is
the examined gift

exercised. I choose
a stone no larger
than my nail, turn

it slowly, remark
by my pelt its trace.
Care intervenes.

3

His gut obstructed
recalls my pledge.
By mouth nil.

Salty vowels drip.
An ice cube
moistens his palate.

Released to sustenance
our words soften
to the familiar.

4

My voice returns
as kindness and I
recover the word

ken—know
three raps for
the acuity of snakes.

We abandon
our tree's desire
at empire's edge

where colonial wild
is neither boy nor girl
nor their swag of nation.

5

When curved light
banners a rain-damp
morning, my camera

feeds the affinity
of friends. Planet
folds this day into

an origami crane.
By evening my ears
overflow with cicadas.

On visiting Elizabeth in the Western Australian Wheatbelt Mary sings a song

after Luke 1:46–55

1

Tyres hold to gravel. She
takes her   breath

sings   each revolution's puff
       of dust. Middle road

a snake suns and wheels' ambit
accommodates her line. Look

back   she chants   see
the reptile still   against

tales she's heard of serpents
clinging to the rim   and found

alive   next stop down
the local access track.

2

All that's left of the school
her nanna ran   and where

married   a lady could
not   hold a teacher's job

is a sign in a paddock. Here
forebears learnt their names.

She reads them now   on
honour boards and on a street

and sings a partway song
of women   white and wanting.

3

This is Ballardong land
where her mother watched

a woman   maybe a girl
work laundry in a copper.

This was a person of Country
in the gaze of a settler child.

She sings recompense
sufficient to the labour

for all unpaid
she lives because.

4

What woman assisted her
nanna   with births at home

on the farm? She sings
their favour   a wisdom

shared on Country   once
more usurped   when a child

is born to inherit. Can
she carol   the

sorry gifts that
made her mother?

5

She psalms a longing
to undo   that cannot

be. She sings to tell
a truth: this colonial

cultivar   this ripped
space   this cleared out

orbit-visible belt whose
indentured labour shames

her family   but does not
threaten their lives. She

takes a breath   sings
out of an old   frontier.

Coda

She stops, she
                listens

Where we sleep

Witness / Cloud Climbers II Print 1/8 by William Kelly

And he dreamed that there was a ladder set up on the earth, the top of it reaching to heaven; and the angels of G-d were ascending and descending on it. (Gen 28:12)

Witness
        Jacob's angels where we sleep   heads pillowed on our
                    ruin

                    This could be any city
                 torched   any two
                          towers straining
    shorter than these steps

             Each
              ladder
                is longer
                    than the
                        next

    (A hand grasps A foot
        grips the News rung
            over our polis

The man in front of the tank
        is tall as the tank
reaches halfway the elevation of the towers
                 quaking
                   (We know about the planes
                      The first is lost
              in fire
                      The second sketched
              in sky

Amid trees   wind fills
               a sovereign flag
          Through bands of black & red

                                   sun
                    breaks
on a man and a tank

and on a single rose
               that scrapes the sky

                         Nearby   a person   palm
                              to hip   stands on a cliff
                                   overlooks the Earth

               Malachei hashalom
                    descend
                         upon our sleep

One sits on cloud
                    edge etched in lead

                         Sky overwhelms the land
                              with hatching strokes

A white gap
               top right   might open to nothing at all
                                   or to a many storied
                                        climb toward

                                   another way
                                        of ground

Afterword

Obligations of voice brings together a selection of poems where the body in its habitat meets the political and social. The first section 'Breathing out' speaks to the obligations of voice in the face of patriarchy, ecological trauma and the vicissitudes of natality and mortality. The second section 'Briefly suddenly' takes up the themes of natality and mortality in poems, engaging with family and friendship, in relation to trauma, grief and embodiment in the cares and habitats that make a home in (un)settled space. The third section 'To write the wind' comprises poems which mostly in third person present a feminist ecological poetics in response to the politics of the academy, border control, invasion, climate change and Covid-19. The fourth and final section 'Where we sleep' includes several longer poems and continues the themes of the previous sections with the addition of resistance to the problematics of patriarchal religion, and imagining the possibility of 'another way of ground'. Each section concludes with the poem from which it takes its title.

Notes

'Grasp': The final two lines are not taken from any other writer, though a google search will show they are common enough and attributed to many speakers.

'Distant calculations': I learnt about 'Poincaré's Universe' in a chapter entitled, 'Geometries other than Euclid's' in W W Sawyer, *Prelude to Mathematics* (Penguin Books, 1955), an extended homage to the beauty, power and joy of mathematics. French Mathematician Henri Poincaré (1854–1912) had described a kind of thought experiment about the mathematical and physical rules that would apply in a two-dimensional world contained in the interior of a circle (pp. 85–88). The italicised words *terrible beauty* are borrowed from W B Yeats, 'Easter 1916', but transferred to the novel coronavirus in 2020 and its material entanglements—political, social, economic, biological.

'Staying with the Grey Sisters at age 3¼': The 'Grey Sisters' refers both to the Family Care Sisters and the Institution they ran in Melbourne to care for children for short periods to give mothers a rest, or if a mother had no one to care for her children during the birth of a sibling.

'Briefly suddenly' is a found poem. The words in the title and the last line come from Martin Harrison, 'A Word' published in *The Best Australian Poems 2009* (Black Inc), the rest in order from his collection *Summer* (Paper Bark Press, 2001).

'At Cana watching Dan and Brett while listening to Michael Farrell read' refers to the biblical narrative of the Wedding at Cana, John 2:1–10, where at his mother's prompt, the Johannine Jesus changes water into wine, and the wedding host escapes the shame of failed hospitality. Dan is Victorian Premier Daniel Andrews and Brett is Victoria's Chief Health Officer Professor Brett Sutton during the second wave of coronavirus in Victoria in July-August 2020.

'Those who sow in tears ...': The full quotation referred to in the epigraph is:

> May those who sow in tears
>
> reap with shouts of joy.   (Psalm 126:5)

'On visiting Elizabeth in the Western Australian Wheatbelt Mary sings a song': The epigraph, 'after Luke 1:46–55', refers to the biblical text of the Magnificat, spoken/sung at the end of the Visitation episode (Luke 1:39–56), when the Lukan Mary, on hearing that her older kinswoman Elizabeth is pregnant, journeys to visit her in the Judean hill country. The poem transfers this journey to the Western Australian Wheatbelt. I first read about the visibility of the Wheatbelt from space in Tony Hughes-d'Aeth, *Like Nothing on this Earth: A Literary History of the Wheatbelt* (UWAP, 2017), p. 1.

'Where we sleep': *Malachei hashalom* is Hebrew for angels (or messengers) of shalom (or peace and wholeness).

Acknowledgements

It is a joy to have this collection published by Recent Work Press, and in particular I thank Shane Strange, whom I met for the first time in person at the Poetry on the Move Festival in 2019. The spirit of the festival, the camaraderie among poets, spring in the ACT, all made the time memorable, and I feel that this book is another link to the wonderful poetry community in Canberra. Thanks to all the locals who made me welcome there for those too-short days.

During the long lockdown in Melbourne's second wave of novel coronavirus in 2020, two local poetry workshops kept bubbling along via Zoom. I thank all the following for their friendship in poetry, insights and encouragement in those workshops: Rose Lucas, Anne M Carson, Phillip Hall, Paul Fleckney, Tom Clark, Jennifer Compton, Gayelene Carbis, Belinda Rule and Emilie Collyer. Warm thanks, also, to Anne Gleeson, Susan Fealy, Michelle Leber, Kate Rigby, Ruth Harrison, Alex Skovron, Peter Boyle and John Eaton, for friendship, inspiration and support of my writing, and to the *Plumwood Mountain* editorial board for all they have taught me about ecological poetry and poetics. To my family, Greg, Matthew, Andrew, Honora, Paul and Marie, Frank and Annette, Monica and Phil, deep appreciation for your love and kindness.

My thanks to the editors who published many of these poems (sometimes in earlier versions) in the following journals, magazines and anthologies:

Anthology of Australian Prose Poetry, *Antipodes*, *Australian Book Review*, *Australian Poetry Journal*, *Australian Poetry Anthology*, *The Blue Nib*, *Cloud Climbers: Words and Images for a Just and Ecologically Sustainable Peace*, *Cordite Poetry Review*, *Demos Journal*, *Dispatches from the Poetry Wars*, *Eureka Street*, *Flash Cove*, *foam:e*, *Have Your Chill*, *Island*, *No News Anthology*, *Not Very Quiet*, *Other Terrain Journal*, *Otoliths*, *Overland*, *Plumwood Mountain*, *Rabbit Poetry Journal*, *Southerly*, *Stilts*, *Transnational Literature*, *Verity La*, *Wasafiri*, *The Weekend Australian Review*, *Westerly*, *What We Carry: An Anthology of Poetry on Childbearing*, *Writing to the Wire*. 'Where we sleep' also appeared in the exhibition *Just Art* by William Kelly, April 25th—June 10th 2019, Pilgrim Theological College, Parkville,

Vic., beside his print *Witness / Cloud Climbers II* to which it is a response. My thanks to William Kelly for his generous insistence that I write in response to his work and for his art itself.

'At Cana watching Dan and Brett while listening to Michael Farrell read' and a version of '(Un-)domesticated settlement' were shortlisted in the 2020 Melbourne Poets Union International Poetry Competition. My thanks to judge Toby Fitch and the MPU administration.

About the author

Anne Elvey lives on BoonWurrung Country in the bayside suburb of Seaford, Victoria. Her poetry publications include: *On arrivals of breath* (Poetica Christi Press, 2019), *White on White* (Cordite Books, 2018), *Intatto. Intact: Ecopoesia. Ecopoetry*, co-authored with Massimo D'Arcangelo and Helen Moore (La Vita Felice, 2017), *This Flesh That You Know* (Leaf Press 2015), international winner of the Overleaf Chapbook Manuscript Award, and *Kin* (Five Islands Press, 2014), which was shortlisted for the Kenneth Slessor Poetry Prize. Her most recent book of research is *Reading the Magnificat in Australia: Unsettling Engagements* (Sheffield Phoenix Press, 2020). She is an Adjunct Research Fellow at Monash University and an Honorary Research Associate at University of Divinity.

www.ingramcontent.com/pod-product-compliance
Ingram Content Group Australia Pty Ltd
76 Discovery Rd, Dandenong South VIC 3175, AU
AUHW020841060325
407965AU00004B/50